Table of Contents

Preface	5
A. Who is God?	7
B. Who is Jesus?	9
C. The Trinity.	17
D. The Bible.	17
E. Creation and the Fall.	19
F. Faith & Justification.	21
G. Gospel & Grace.	23
H. Eternal Life.	23
I. The Kingdom.	25
J. The New Covenant.	27
K. The Local Assembly.	31
L. The Ordinances.	35
M. Magistrates.	39

The

CONFESSION OF FAITH

Of those Congregations which are commonly (though falsely) called

ANABAPTISTS

Organized by topic with additional articles on the Lord's Supper

Presented to the view of all that fear God, to examine by the touchstone of the Word of Truth;

As likewise for the

taking off those aspersions which are frequently both in

Pulpit and Print,

(although unjustly) cast upon them.

Acts 4. 20
We cannot but speak the things which we have seen and heard.

Isai. 8. 20
To the Law and to the testimony, if they speak not according to this Rule, it is because there is no light in them.

2 Cor. 1. 9,10
But we had the sentence of death in ourselves, that we should not trust in ourselves, but in the living God, which raises the dead; who delivered us from so great a death, and does deliver, in whom we trust that he will yet deliver.

London

Printed in the year of our Lord,

1644

Brogden's Books
http://reformedbaptistlibrary.tk/Books.html
brogdensbooks@gmail.com
La Vernia, TX 78121

Baptist Reprints, book #3, revision 2

Reprint, 2020

Preface

TO ALL THAT DESIRE

The Lifting up of the Name of the LORD JESUS in sincerity, the poor despised assemblies of God in London send greeting, with prayers for their farther increase in the knowledge of CHRIST JESUS.

We admit that it will seem strange to many men that such as we are (frequently termed to be lying under that calumny and black brand of heretics, and sowers of division as we do) should presume to appear so publicly as now we have done. But yet notwithstanding we may well say, to give answer to such, what David said to his brethren, when the Lord's battle was a fighting. I Sam. 29:30. Is there not a cause? Surely, if ever people had cause to speak for the vindication of the truth of Christ in their hands, we have, that being indeed the mail wheel at this time that sets us a work. For had anything by men been transacted against our persons only, we could quietly have sit still, and committed our cause to Him who is a righteous Judge, who will in the great day judge the secrets of all men's hearts by Jesus Christ. But being it is not only us, but the truth professed by us, we cannot, we dare not but speak. It is no strange thing to any observing man, what sad charges are laid, not only by the world that know not God, but also by those that think themselves much wronged, if they be not looked upon as the chief worthies of the body of God, and watchmen of the city. But it has fared with us from them as from the poor spouse seeking her beloved. They finding us out of that common roadway themselves walk, have smote us and taken away our veil, that so we may by them be odious in the eyes of all that behold us, and in the hearts of all that think upon us, which they have done both in pulpit and print, charging us with holding free will, falling away from grace, denying original sin, disclaiming of magistracy, denying to assist them either in persons or purse, in any of their lawful commands, being acts unseemly in the dispensing the ordinance of baptism, not to be named amongst Christians. All which charges we disclaim as notoriously untrue, though, by reason of these calumnies cast upon us, many that fear God are discouraged and forestalled in harboring a good thought, either of us or what we profess; and many that know not God encouraged, if they can find the place of our meeting, to get together in clusters to stone us, as looking upon us as a people holding such things, as that we are not worthy to live.

We have, therefore, for the clearing of the truth we profess, that it may be at liberty though we be in bonds, briefly published a confession of our faith, as desiring all that fear God, seriously to consider, whether (if they compare what we here say and confess, in the presence of the Lord Jesus and His saints) men have not with their tongues in pulpit, and pens in print, both spoken and written things that are contrary to truth. But we know our God in His own time will clear our cause, and lift up His Son to make Him the chief corner stone, though He has been (or now should be) rejected of master builders. And because it may be conceived, that what is here published may be but the judgment of some one particular congregation, more refined than the rest, we do therefore here subscribe it, some of each body in the name, and by the appointment of seven congregations; who, though we be distinct in respect of our particular bodies, for convenience sake, being as many as can well meet together in one place, yet are all in communion holding Jesus Christ to be our Head and Lord; under whose government we desire alone to walk, in the following the Lamb wherever He goes. And we believe the Lord will daily cause truth more to appear in the hearts of His saints, and make them ashamed of their folly in the land of their nativity, that so they may, with one shoulder, more study to lift up the name of the Lord Jesus, and stand for His appointments and laws; which is the desire and prayers of the contemned Churches of Christ in London for all saints.

Subscribed in the Names of seven Churches in London:

William Kiffen	Thomas Killcop	Thomas Patience
John Webb	John Spilsbery	Paul Hobson
George Tipping	Thomas Goare	Samuel Richardson
Thomas Munday	Joseph Phelpes	Thomas Skippard
Edward Heath	Thomas Gunne	John Mabbitt

THE CONFESSION OF FAITH

of those Congregations which are commonly (though falsely) called

ANABAPTISTS.

A. Who is God?

Article 1. God as He is in Himself, cannot be comprehended of any but Himself, dwelling in that inaccessible light, that no eye can attain unto, whom man has never looked upon, nor can see; that there is but one God, one Christ, one Spirit, one Faith, one Baptism; one Rule of holiness and obedience for all Saints, at all times, in all places to be observed.

I Tim. 6:16; I Tim. 2:5; Eph. 4:4, 5, 6; I Cor. 12:4, 5 ,6, 13; John 14, chap. 6; I Tim. 6:3,13,14; Gal. 1:8,9; 2 Tim. 3:15-17.

Article 2. God is of Himself, that is, neither from another, nor of another, nor by another, nor for another; but is a Spirit, Who as His being is of Himself, so He gives being, moving, and preservation to all other things, being in Himself, eternal, most holy, every way infinite in greatness, wisdom, power, justice, goodness, truth, etc. In this God-head, there is the Father, the Son, and the Spirit; being every one of them one and the same God; and therefore, not divided, but distinguished one from another by their several persons; the Father being from

Himself, the Son of the Father from everlasting, the Holy Spirit proceeding from the Father and the Son.

Isa. 44:67 and 43:11 and 46:9; John 4:24; Exod. 3:14; Rom. 11:36; Acts 17:28; I Cor. 8:6; Pro. 8:22, 23; Heb. 1:3; John 1:18. John 15:26; Gal. 4:6.

Article 3. God has decreed in Himself from everlasting touching all things, effectually to work and dispose them according to the counsel of His own will, to the glory of His Name; in which decree appears His wisdom, constancy, truth, and faithfulness. Wisdom is that whereby He contrives all things. Constancy is that whereby the decree of God remains always immutable. Truth is that whereby He declares that alone which He has decreed, and though His sayings may seem to sound sometimes another thing, yet the sense of them does always agree with the decree. Faithfulness is that whereby He effects that He has decreed, as He has decreed. And touching His creature man, God had in Christ before the foundation of the world, according to the good pleasure of His will, foreordained some men to eternal life through Jesus Christ, to the praise and glory of His grace, leaving the rest in their sin to their just condemnation, to the praise of His Justice.

Isa. 45:10; Rom. 11:34, 35, 36; Mat. 10:29, 30; Eph. 1:11. Col. 2:35; Num. 13:19, 20; Jere. 10:10; Rom. 3:4; Isa. 44:10; Eph. 1:3, 4, 5,

6, 7; 2 Tim. 1:9; Acts 13:48; Rom. 8:28, 29; Jude ver. 4 & 6; Rom.9:11, 12, 13.; Prov. 16:4.

B. Who is Jesus?

Article 4. Regarding the Lord Jesus, of whom Moses and the Prophets wrote, and whom the Apostles preached, He is the Son of God the Father, the brightness of His glory, the engraved form of His being, God with Him and with His Holy Spirit, by Whom He made the world, by Whom He upholds and governs all the work He has made. Who also, when the fullness of time was come, was made man of a woman, of the Tribe of Judah, of the seed of Abraham and David, to wit, of Mary that blessed Virgin, by the Holy Spirit coming upon her, and the power of the most High overshadowing her, and was also in all things like unto us, but without sin.

Gen. 3:15 & 22, 18, & 49:10. Dan. 7:13 & 9:14, 25, 26. Prov. 8: 23; John 1: 1, 2, 3; Col. 1: 1,15,16,17. Gal. 4:4. Heb. 7:14; Rev. 5:5 with Gen. 49:9, 10; Rom. 1:3, & 9:5. Matt. 1:46 with Luke 3:23, 26. Heb. 2:10; Isa. 53: 3, 4, 5; Phil. 2:8.

Article 5. Regarding His Office, Jesus Christ only is made the Mediator of the New Covenant that unites God and Man, to be perfectly and fully the Prophet, Priest and King of the Church of God for evermore.

2 Tim. 2:15; Heb. 9:15; John 14:6; Heb. 1:2 & 3:1, 2 & 7:4; Isa. 9: 6, 7; Acts 5:31.

Article 6. Unto this Office He was foreordained from everlasting, by the authority of the Father, and in respect of His Manhood, from the womb called and separated, and anointed also most fully and abundantly with all gifts necessary, God having without measure poured the Spirit upon Him.

Prov. 8:23; Isa. 41:6 & 49:1,5; Isa. 11:2, 3, 4, 5 & 61: 1,2,3; Luke 4:17, 22; John 1:14, 16 & 3:34.

Article 7. In this Call the Scripture holds forth two special things considerable; first, the call to the Office; secondly, the Office itself. First, that none takes this honor but He that is called of God, as was Aaron, so also Christ, it being an action especially of God the Father, whereby a special covenant being made, He ordains His Son to this office: which Covenant is, that Christ should be made a Sacrifice for sin, that He shall see His seed, and prolong His days, and the pleasure of the Lord shall prosper in His hand; which calling therefore contains in itself choosing, ordaining, sending. Choosing respects the end, foreordaining the means, sending the execution itself, all of mere grace, without any condition fore-seen, either in men, or in Christ Himself.

Heb. 5:4,5,6; Isa. 53:10,11; Isa. 42:18; I Pet. 1:20; John 3:17 & 9:27; & 10:36; Isa. 61:1; John 3:16; Rom. 8:32.

Article 8. So that this Office to be Mediator, that is, to be Prophet, Priest, and King of the Church of God, is so proper to Christ, as neither in the whole, nor in any part thereof, it can be transferred from Him to any other.

I Tim. 2:5; Heb. 7:24; Dan. 7:14; Acts 4:13; Luke 1:33; John 14:6.

Article 9. This Office itself to which Christ was called, is threefold, of a Prophet, of Priest, & of a King: this number and order of Offices is showed; first, by men's necessities grievously laboring under ignorance, by reason whereof they stand in infinite necessity of the Prophetical office of Christ to relieve them. Secondly, alienation from God, wherein they stand in need of the Priestly Office to reconcile them. Thirdly, our utter disability to return to Him, by which they stand in need of the power of Christ in His Kingly Office to assist and govern them.

Deut. 18:15, with Acts 3:22, 23; Psal. 110:3; Heb. 3:1 & 4:14-15 & 5:6 & 21; Psa. 2:6; Acts 26:18; Col. 1:3; Col. 1:21; Eph. 2:12; John 6:44.

Article 10. Regarding the Prophecy of Christ, it is that whereby He has perfectly revealed the whole will of God out of the bosom of the Father, that is needful for His servants to know, believe, and obey; and therefore is called not only a Prophet and a Doctor, and the Apostle of our profession, and the Angel of the Covenant; but also the very wisdom of God, and the treasures of wisdom and understanding.

John 1:18, & 12:49, 50 & 15 & 17:8; Deut. 18:15; Mat. 23:10; Heb. 3:1; Mal. 3:1; I Cor. 1:24; Col. 2:3.

Article 11. That He might be such a Prophet as thereby to be every way complete, it was necessary that He should be God, and withal also that He should be man. For unless He had been God, He could never have perfectly understood the will of God, neither had He been able to reveal it throughout all ages. And unless He had been man, He could not have properly unfolded it in His own person to man.

John 1:18 & 3:13; I Cor. 2:11, 16; Acts 3:22 with Deut. 18:15; Heb. 1:1.

Article 12. Regarding His Priesthood, Christ being consecrated, has appeared once to put away sin by the offering and sacrifice of Himself, and to this end has fully performed and suffered all those things by which God, through the blood of that His cross in an acceptable sacrifice, might reconcile His elect only. Having broken down the partition wall, and therewith finished and removed all those Rites, Shadows and Ceremonies, is now entered within the Veil, into the Holy of Holies, that is, to the very Heavens and presence of God, where He forever lives and sits at the right hand of Majesty, appearing before the face of His Father to make intercession for such as come to the Throne of Grace by that new and living way. Furthermore, He makes His people a spiritual House, an holy Priesthood, to offer up spiritual sacrifice acceptable to God through Him. Lastly, neither does the Father accept, nor Christ offer to the Father any other worship or worshippers.

John 17:19; Heb. 5:7, 8, 9, & 9:26; Rom. 5:19; Eph. 5:2; Col. 1:20; Eph. 1:14, 15, 16; Rom. 8:14; I Pet.1:5; John 4:23, 24.

Article 13. This Priesthood was not legal, or temporary, but according to the order of Melchizedek; not by a carnal commandment, but by the power of an endless life; not by an order that is weak and lame, but stable and perfect; not for a time, but forever, admitting no successor, but perpetual and proper to Christ, and of Him that ever lives. Christ Himself was the Priest, Sacrifice and Altar. He was Priest, according to both natures, He was a sacrifice most properly according to His human nature; whence in the Scripture it is there to be attributed to His body, to His blood. Yet the chief force whereby this sacrifice was made effectual, did depend upon His divine nature, namely, that the Son of God did offer Himself for us. He was the Altar properly according to His divine nature, it belonging to the Altar to sanctify that which is offered upon it, and so it ought to be of greater dignity than the Sacrifice itself.

Heb. 7:17; Heb. 7:16; Heb. 7:18, 19, 20, 21; Heb. 7:24, 25; Heb. 5:6; Heb. 10:16; I Pet. 1:18, 19; Col. 1:20, 22; Isa. 53:10; Matt. 20:28. Acts 20:28; Rom. 8:3; Heb. 9:14, & 13: 10, 12, 15; Matt. 23:17; John 17:19.

Article 14. Regarding His Kingdom, Christ being risen from the dead, ascended into heaven, sat on the right hand of God the Father, having all power in heaven and earth, given unto Him, He does spiritually govern His people. He exercises His power over all Angels and Men, good and bad, to the preservation and salvation of the elect, to the overruling and destruction of His enemies, which are the Reprobates. He applies the benefits, virtue, and fruit of His Prophecy and Priesthood to His elect; namely, to the subduing and taking away of their sins, to their justification and adoption of Sons, regeneration, sanctification, preservation and strengthening in all their conflicts against Satan, the World, the Flesh, and the temptations of them. He continually dwells within, governing and keeping their hearts in faith and filial fear by His Spirit, which having given it, He never takes away from them. By the Spirit He still begets and nourishes in them faith, repentance, love, joy, hope, and all heavenly light in the soul unto immortality, notwithstanding through our own unbelief, and temptations of Satan, the sensible sight of this light and love be clouded and overwhelmed for the time. And on the contrary, ruling in the world over His enemies, Satan, and all the vessels of wrath, limiting, using, restraining them by His mighty power, as seems good in His divine wisdom & justice to the execution of His determinate counsel, delivering them up to a reprobate mind, to be kept through their own deserts, in darkness and sensuality unto judgment.

I Cor. 15:4; I Pet. 3:21, 22; Mat. 28:18, 19, 20; Luke 24:51; Acts 1:11 & 5:30, 31; John 19:36; Rom. 14:17; Mark 1:27; Heb. 1:14; Jn. 16:7,15; John 5:26, 27; Rom. 5:6, 7, 8 & 14:17; Gal. 5:22, 23; John 1:4, 13; John 13:1 & 10:28, 29, & 14:16, 17; Rom. 11:29; Psa. 51:10, 11; Job 33:29, 30; 2 Cor. 12:7,9; Job 1 and 2; Rom. 1:21 & 2:4,5,6, & 9:17,18. Eph. 4:17, 18; 2 Pet. 3 chap.

Article 15. Jesus Christ, by His death, did bring forth salvation and reconciliation only for the elect, which were those which God the Father gave him. That the Gospel which is to be preached to all men as the ground of faith, is that Jesus is the Christ, the Son of the ever blessed God, filled with the perfection of all heavenly and spiritual excellencies, and that salvation is only and alone to be had through the believing in His Name.

    John 15:13; Rom. 8:32, 33, 34; Rom. 5:11 & 3:25; John 17:2 with 6:37; Matt. 16:16; Luke 2:26; Matt. 16:16. Luke 2:26; Joh. 6:9 & 7: 3 & 20:32; I John 5:11.

C. The Trinity.

Article 16. God the Father, and Son, and Spirit, is one with all believers, in their fullness, in relations, as head and members, as house and inhabitants, as husband and wife, one with Him, as light and love, and one with Him in His inheritance, and in all His glory. All believes by virtue of this union and oneness with God, are the adopted sons of God, and heirs with Christ, co-heirs and joint-heirs with Him of the inheritance of all the promises of this life, and that which is to come.

I Thes. 1:1; John 14:10, 12 & 17:21; Col. 2:9, 10. & 1:19; John 1:17; John 20:17; Heb. 2:11; Col. 1:18; Eph. 2:12; Cor. 3:16, 17; Isa. 16:5; 2 Cor. 11:3; Gal. 3:16; John 17:24.

D. The Bible.

Article 17. The rule of this Knowledge, Faith, and Obedience, concerning the worship and service of God, and all other Christian duties, is not man's inventions, opinions, devices, laws, constitutions, or traditions unwritten whatsoever, but only the Word of God contained in the Canonical Scriptures.

John 5:39; 2 Tim. 3:15, 16, 17; Col. 2:18, 23; Matt. 15:9.

Article 18. In this written Word God has plainly revealed whatsoever He has thought needful for us to know, believe, and acknowledge, concerning the Nature and Office of Christ, in whom all the promises are Yes and Amen to the praise of God.

    Acts 3: 22.23; Heb. 1:1, 2; 2 Tim. 3:15, 16, 17; 2 Co. 1:29.

E. Creation and the Fall.

Article 19. In the beginning God made all things very good, created man after His own Image and likeness, filling him with all perfection of all natural excellence and uprightness, free from all sin. But long he abode not in this honor, but by the subtlety of the Serpent, which Satan used as his instrument, himself with his Angels having sinned before, and not kept their first estate, but left their own habitation; first Eve, then Adam being seduced did wittingly and willingly fall into disobedience and transgression of the Commandment of their great Creator, for the which death came upon all, and reigned over all, so that all since the Fall are conceived in sin, and brought forth in iniquity, and so by nature children of wrath, and servants of sin, subjects of death, and all other calamities due to sin in this world and forever, being considered in the state of nature, without relation to Christ.

Gen. 1; Col. 1:16; Heb. 11:3; Isa. 45:12; Gen. 1:26; I Cor. 15:45,46; Eccles. 7:31; Psal.49:10; Gen. 3:1,4,5; 2 Cor. 11:3; 2 Pet. 2:4; Jude 6; John 6:44; Gen. 3:1,2,6; I Tim. 2:14; Eccles.7:31; Gal. 3:22; Rom. 5:12,18,19; & 6,23; Eph. 2:3.

Article 20. All mankind being fallen and become altogether dead in sins and trespasses, and subjects to the eternal wrath of the great

God by transgression; yet the elect, which God has loved with an everlasting love, are redeemed, quickened, and saved, not by themselves, neither by their own works, lest any man should boast of himself; but wholly and only by God of His free grace and mercy through Jesus Christ, who of God is made unto us wisdom, righteousness, sanctification and redemption, that as it is written, He that rejoices, let him rejoice in the Lord.

Jer. 31:3. Gen. 3:15; Eph. 1:3, 7, & 2, 4 ,9; I Thess. 5:9; Acts 13:: 38. I Cor. 1:30, 31; 2 Cor. 5:21; Jer. 9::23, 24.

F. Faith & Justification.

Article 21. Faith is the gift of God wrought in the hearts of the elect by the Spirit of God, whereby they come to see, know, and believe the truth of the Scriptures, and the excellence of them above all other writings and things in the world. The Scriptures alone hold forth the glory of God in His attributes, the excellence of Christ in His nature and offices, and the power of the fullest of the Spirit in its workings and operations. By this faith, the saints are enabled to cast the weight of their souls upon this truth thus believed.

Eph. 2:8; John 6:29 & 4:10; Phil. 1:29; Gal. 5:22; John 7:17; Heb. 4:11, 12; John 6:63.

Article 22. Those that have this precious faith wrought in them by the Spirit can never finally nor totally fall away; though many storms and floods will arise and beat against them, yet they shall never be moved off that foundation and rock which by faith they are fastened upon, but shall be kept by the power of God to salvation, where they shall enjoy their purchased possession, they being formally engraved upon the palms of God's hands.

Matt. 7:24, 25; John 13:1; I Pet. 1: 4, 5, 6; Isa. 49: 13, 14, 15, 6.

Article 23. Faith is ordinarily begot by the preaching of the Gospel, or word of Christ, without respect to any power or capacity in the creature, but it is wholly passive, being dead in sins and trespasses, does believe, and is converted by no less power than that which raised Christ from the dead.

Rom. 10:17; I Cor. 1:21; Rom. 9:16; Rom. 2:1, 2; Ezek. 16:6; Rom. 3:12; Rom. 1:16; Eph. 1:19; Col. 2:12.

G. Gospel & Grace.

Article 24. The proclamation of the Gospel for the conversion of sinners is absolutely free, no way requiring as absolutely necessary, any qualifications, preparations, terrors of the Law, or preceding Ministry of the Law, but only and alone the naked soul, as a sinner and ungodly to receive Christ, as crucified, dead and buried, and risen again, being made a Prince and a Savior for such sinners.

John 3:14, 15 & 1:12; Isa. 55:1; John 7:37; I Tim. 1:15; Rom. 4:5. & 5:8; Act 5:30, 31 & 2:36; I Cor. 1:22, 23, 24.

Article 25. The same power that converts to faith in Christ, the same power carries on the soul still through all duties, temptations, conflicts, sufferings, and continually whatever a Christian is, he is by grace, and by a constant renewed operation from God, without which he cannot perform any duty to God, or undergo any temptations from Satan, the world, or men.

I Pet. 1:5; 2 Cor. 12:9; I Cor. 15:10; Phil. 2:12, 13; John 15:5; Gal. 1: 19, 20.

H. Eternal Life.

Article 26. This is life eternal, to know the only true God, and Whom He has sent Jesus Christ. And on the contrary, the Lord will render vengeance in flaming fire to them that know not

God and obey not the Gospel of our Lord Jesus Christ.

>John 17:3; Heb. 5:9; Jer. 23:5, 6. 2 Thess. 1:8; John 3:36.

I. The Kingdom.

Article 27. This Kingdom shall be then fully consummated when He returns the second time, in glory, to reign among His Saints, and to be admired of all them which do believe. He shall put down all rule and authority under His feet, so the glory of the Father may be full and perfectly manifested in His Son, and the glory of the Father and the Son in all His members.

I Cor. 15:24, 28; Matt. 9:28; I Thess. 1:9, 10; 1 Thess. 4:15, 16, 17; John 17: 21, 26.

Article 28. Christ has here on earth a spiritual Kingdom, the Church, which He has purchased and redeemed to Himself, a peculiar inheritance. The Church, as it is visible to us, is a company of visible Saints, called & separated from the world, by the word and Spirit of God, to the visible profession of the faith of the Gospel, being baptized into that faith, and joined to the Lord, and each other, by mutual agreement, in the practical enjoyment of the Ordinances, commanded by Christ their head and King.

I Cor. 1:1; Eph. 1:1; Rom. 1:7; Acts 16:18; I Thess 1:9; 2 Cor. 6:17; Rev. 18:18; Acts 2:37 with Acts 10:17; Rom. 10:10; Acts 20:28; Mark 16:19, 20; Acts 2:41; I Pet. 2:5.

J. The New Covenant.

Article 29. Those which have union with Christ are justified from all their sins, past, present, and to come, by the blood of Christ. This justification we conceive to be a gracious and free acquaintance of a guilty, sinful creature, from all sin by God, through the satisfaction that Christ has made by His death; and this applied in the manifestation of it through faith.

I John 1:7; Heb. 10:14; & 9:26; 2 Cor. 5:19; Rom. 3:21; Acts 13:38, 39; Rom. 5:1. & 3:25, 30.

Article 30. All believers are a holy and sanctified people, and that sanctification is a spiritual grace of the New Covenant, and effect of the love of God, manifested to the soul, whereby the believer is in truth and reality separated, both in soul and body, from all sin and dead works, through the blood of the everlasting Covenant, whereby he also presses after a heavenly and evangelical perfection, in obedience to all the Commands, which Christ as head and King in this New Covenant has prescribed to Him.

I Cor. 1:1; I Pet. 2:9; Eph. 1:4; I John 4:16; Eph. 4:24; Phil. 3:15; Mat. 28:20.

Article 31. All believers through the knowledge of that Justification of life given by the Father and brought forth by the blood of Christ, have this as their great privilege of that New Covenant: peace with God, and reconciliation, whereby they that were afar off, were brought nigh by that blood, and have (as the Scripture speaks) peace passing all understanding, yea, joy in God, through our Lord Jesus Christ, by whom we have received the Atonement.

2 Cor. 5:19; Rom. 5:9, 10; Isa. 54:10; & 26:12; Eph. 2:13, 14; Phil. 4:7; Rom. 5:10, 11.

Article 32. All believers in the time of this life, are in a continual warfare, combat, and opposition against sin, self, the world, and the Devil; liable to all manner of afflictions, tribulations, and persecutions. This shall continue until Christ comes to consummate His Kingdom, being predestinated and appointed for this. Whatsoever the Saints, any of them do profess or enjoy of God in this life, is only by faith.

Eph. 6:10, 11, 12, 13; 2 Cor. 10:3; Rev. 2:9, 10.

Article 33. The only strength by which the Saints are enabled to encounter with all opposition, and to overcome all afflictions, temptations, persecutions, and trials is only by Jesus Christ. He is the Captain of their salvation, being made perfect through sufferings, who has engaged His strength to assist them in all their afflictions, and to uphold them under all their temptations, and to preserve them by His power to His everlasting Kingdom.

John 16:33; Heb. 1:9, 10; John 15:5.

Article 34. To this chosen people He has made His promises, and given the signs of His Covenant, presence, love, blessing, and protection. Here are the fountains and springs of His heavenly grace continually flowing forth, by which men will come, of all estates, that acknowledge Him to be their Prophet, Priest, and King, to be enrolled amongst His household servants, to be under His heavenly conduct and government, to lead their lives in His walled sheepfold, and watered garden, to have communion here with the Saints, that they may be made to be partakers of their inheritance in the Kingdom of God.

Mat. 28:18, 19, 20; 2 Cor. 6:18; Isa. 8:16; 1 Tim. 3:15 & 4:16, & 6:3,5; Acts 2:4147; Song 4:12; Gal. 6:10; Eph. 2:19.

Article 35. All His servants are called to present their bodies and souls to God, and to bring their gifts God has given them. They are there by Himself bestowed in their several order, peculiar place, due use, being fitly compact and knit together, according to the effectual working of every part, to the edification of itself in love.

I Cor. 12:6, 7, 12, 18; Rom. 12:4, 5, 6; I Pet. 4:10; Eph. 4:16; Col. 2:5, 6, 19; I Cor. 12.

K. The Local Assembly.

Article 36. Being thus joined, every congregation has power given them from Christ for their better well-being, to choose to themselves qualified persons into the office of Elders and Deacons. Those who are qualified according to the Word as those which Christ has appointed in His Testament, for the feeding, governing, serving, and building up of His body, and that none other have power to impose them, either these or any other.

Acts 6:6; with 15:22, 25; Rom. 12:7, 8; I Tim. 3:2, 6, 7, 8; I Cor. 12: 8, 28; Heb. 13:7, 17; I Pet. 5:1, 2, 3; I Pet. 4:15.

Article 37. The Ministers mentioned above, lawfully called by the congregation, where they are to administer, ought to continue in their calling, according to God's Ordinance, and carefully to feed the flock of Christ committed to them, not for greedy motives, but of a ready mind.

Heb. 5:4; John 10:3, 4; Acts 20:28, 29; Rom. 12:7,8; Heb. 3:7, 17; I Pet. 5:1, 2, 3.

Article 38. The due maintenance of the Officers mentioned should be the free and voluntary support of the local assembly. According to Christ's Ordinance, they that preach the

Gospel, should live of the Gospel, and not by constraint, to be compelled from the people by a forced Law.

I Cor. 9:7, 14; Gal. 6:6; Phil. 4:15, 16; 1 Tim 1:12.

Article 39. Christ has also given power to each local congregation to receive in and cast out, by way of Excommunication, any unrepentant member. This power is given to every particular congregation, and not one particular person, either member or Officer, but the whole.

Acts 2:47; Rom. 16:1; Matt. 18:17; I Cor. 5:4; 2 Cor. 2:6, 7, 8.

Article 40. Every particular member of each congregation, no matter how excellent, great, or learned, ought to be subject to this censure and judgment of Christ; and the congregation ought with great care and tenderness, with due advice to proceed against her members.

Matt. 18:17; Acts 11:2, 3; I Tim. 5:19, 20, 21.

Article 41. As for Christ keeping His Church in holy and orderly Communion, places some special men over the congregation, who by their office are to govern, observe, visit, watch; so likewise for the better keeping thereof in all places, by the members, He has given authority, and laid duty upon all, to watch over one another. This means the elders are not removed from accountability within the local fellowship.

Acts 20:27, 28; Heb. 13:17, 24; Matt. 24:24; I Thess. 5:14; Mark 13:34-37; Gal. 6:1; I Thess. 5:12, 13; Jude 3, 20; Heb. 10:24, 25; & 12:15.

Article 42. To whom God has given gifts, being tested within the congregation, may and should, by the appointment of the Congregation, to prophesy, according to the proportion of faith, and so to teach publicly the Word of God for the edification, exhortation, and comfort of the assembly of saints.

I Cor. 14; Rom. 12:6; I Pet. 4:10, 11; I Cor. 12:7; 1 Thess. 5:17, 18, 19.

Article 43. Being rightly gathered, established, and proceeding in Christian communion, and obedience of the Gospel of Christ, none ought to separate for faults and corruptions, which may, and as long as the congregation consists of men subject to failings, will fall out and arise amongst them, even in true constituted Churches, until they have in due order sought reconciliation.

Rev. 2 & 3 chapters; Acts 15:1,2; I Cor. 1:10; Eph. 2:16 & 3:15,16; Heb. 10:25; Jude 19; Matt. 18;19; I Cor. 5:2, 4, 5.

Article 44. Although the particular congregations be distinct and several bodies, every one as a compact and knit fellowship in itself; yet are they all to walk by one and the same Rule, and by all means to have the counsel and help one of another in all needful affairs of the Church, as members of one body in the common faith under Christ their only head.

I Cor. 4:17 & 14:31, 36 & 16:1; Matt. 28:20; 2 Tim. 3:15; & 6:13, 14; Rev. 22:18, 19; Col. 2:6, 19 & 4:16.

L. The Ordinances.

The Lord God has seen fit to give His people two ordinance to remind them in picture form the great act of grace that saved them and the promise of Christ Jesus to come back for them

Article 45. The persons designed by Christ to dispense these ordinances are shown in the Scriptures to be a preaching Disciple. It is nowhere tied to a particular Church, Office, or person extraordinarily sent to administer the Commission. The administration being given to those under no other consideration but as those considered Disciples.

      Matt. 28:16-19; John 4:1, 2; 1 Cor 1:17.

Water Baptism

Article 46. Baptism is an Ordinance of the New Covenant, given by Christ, to be administered only to persons professing faith, are Disciples, or taught; who, upon a profession of faith, ought to be baptized.

      Matt. 28:18, 19; John 4:1; Mark 16:15, 16; Acts 2:37, 38, and 8:36, 37, 38; & 18:8.

Article 47. The way and manner of the dispensing of this Ordinance is revealed in the Scripture to be dipping or plunging the whole body under water. Being a sign, it must answer the thing signified, which are these: first, the washing the whole soul in the blood of Christ: second, that interest the Saints have in the death, burial, and resurrection; third, together with a confirmation of our faith, that as certainly as the body is buried under water, and rises again, so certainly shall the bodies of the Saints be raised by the power of Christ, in the day of the resurrection, to reign with Christ. The word Baptize, signifying to dip under water, with proper garments both upon the administrator and subject with all modesty.

Matt. 3:16; Mark 1:9; John 3:25; Acts 8:38; Rev. 1:5; & 7:14; with Heb. 10:22; Rom. 6:3, 4, 5; I Cor. 15:28, 29.

The Lord's Supper

Article 48. The Lord's Supper an Ordinance of the New Covenant, given by Christ, to be administered only to persons professing faith, are Disciples who spiritually receive, and feed upon Christ crucified, with all the benefits of his death; the body and blood of Christ being then not corporally or carnally, but spiritually present to the faith of believers. Ignorant and ungodly persons, as they are unfit to enjoy communion with Christ, so are they unworthy of the Lord's table, and cannot, without great sin against him, while they remain such, partake of these holy mysteries, or be admitted thereunto. Yea, whosoever shall receive unworthily, are guilty of the body and blood of the Lord, eating and drinking judgment to themselves.

1 Cor. 11:23-26; 1 Cor. 10:16,17,21; 2 Cor. 6:14,15; 1 Cor. 11:29; Matt. 7:6.

Article 49. The reason this ordinance was given to the church is to declare the death of Christ; that He did die for the sins of His people; to demonstrate the manner of His death, by crucifixion; by his being pierced, wounded, bruised, and broken; and to express the blessings and benefits of his death, and the faith of his people in Him, and thankfulness for His obedience. Further, we proclaim His death until returns; this reminds us that Jesus has gone to prepare a place for us and has promised to return to take us to be with Himself for eternity.

Heb. 10:12-14; John 1:29; John 14:3

M. Magistrates.

Article 50. Civil Magistrates are set up by God for the punishment of evil doers and for the praise of them that do well, and that in all lawful things commanded by them, men are to be subject to them, as commanded by the Lord. We are to make supplication and prayer for Kings, and all that are in authority, that under them we may live a peaceable and quiet life in all godliness and honesty.

Rom. 13:1, 2, 3, 4; I Peter 2:13, 14; I Tim. 2:2.

Article 51. The supreme Magistrate of this Kingdom we believe to be the political leaders freely chosen by the Kingdom, and that in all those civil Laws which have been acted by them, or for the present is or shall be ordained, we are bound to yield subjection and obedience unto in the Lord, as conceiving ourselves bound to defend both the persons of those thus chosen, and all civil Laws made by them, with our persons, liberties, and estates, with all that is called ours, although we should suffer never so much from them in not actively submitting to some Ecclesiastical Laws, which might be conceived by them to be their duties to establish, which we for the present could not see, nor our consciences could submit unto; yet are we bound to yield our persons to their pleasures.

Rom. 12:18

Article 52. If God should provide such a mercy for us as to influence the Magistrates' hearts to be tender towards our consciences, that we might be protected by them from wrong, injury, oppression and molestation. We formerly have groaned under by the tyranny and oppression of worldly hierarchy; though God through mercy has made this present government wonderfully honorable, as an instrument in His hand, to throw down. We thereby have had some breathing time, we shall, we hope, look at it as a mercy beyond our expectation, and conceive ourselves further engaged for ever to bless God for it.

I Tim. 1:2, 3, 4; Psa. 116:1; Acts 9:31.

Article 53. If God with-hold the Magistrates' allowance and furtherance herein; yet we must notwithstanding proceed together in Christian communion, not daring to suspend our practice, but to walk in obedience to Christ in the profession and holding forth this faith, even in the midst of all trials and afflictions, nor accounting our goods, lands, wives, children, fathers, mothers, brethren, sisters, yea, and our own lives dear unto us, so we may finish our course with joy. We need to always remember that we are to obey God rather than men, and standing on the commandment, commission and promise of our Lord and master Jesus Christ, who as He has all power in heaven and earth, so also has promised, if we keep His commandments which he has given us, to be with us to the end of the world. When we have finished our course, and kept the faith, to give us the crown of righteousness, which is laid up for all that love His appearing, and to whom we must give an account of all our actions, no man being able to discharge us of the same.

Acts 2:40, 41 & 4:19 & 5:28 & 19:41 & 20:23; I Thess. 3:3; Phil. 1:27-29; Dan. 3:16, 17; 6:7, 10, 22, 23; Matt. 28:18-20; I Tim. 6:13-15; Rom. 12:1,8; I Cor. 14:17; 2 Tim. 4:7, 8; Rev. 2:20; Gal. 2:4, 5.

Article 54. Likewise unto all men is to be given whatsoever is their due; tributes, customs, and all such lawful duties, should willingly be by us paid and performed, our lands, goods, and bodies, to submit to the Magistrate in the Lord, and the Magistrate every way to be acknowledged, reverenced, and obeyed, according to godliness; not because of wrath only, but for conscience sake. And finally, all men so to be esteemed and regarded, as is due and meet for their place, age, estate and condition.

Rom. 13:5, 6, 7; Matt. 22:21; Titus 3; 2 Pet. 2:13; Eph. 5:21, 22 & 6:1, 9; I Pet. 5:5; 1 Cor 5:10.

Article 55. So, then, we desire to give unto God that which is God's, and unto Caesar that which is Caesar's, and unto all men that which belongs unto them, endeavoring ourselves to have always a clear conscience void of offense towards God, and towards man. And if any take this that we have said, to be heresy, then we with the Apostle freely confess, that after the way which they call heresy, worship we the God of our Fathers, believing all things which are written in the Law and in the Prophets and Apostles, desiring from our souls to disclaim all heresies and opinions which are not after Christ, and to be steadfast, unmovable, always abounding in the work of the Lord, as knowing our labor shall not be in vain in the Lord.

Matt. 22:21; Acts 23:14 - 16; John 5:28.

I Cor. 1: 24 Not that we have dominion over your faith, but are helpers of your joy: for by faith we stand.

FINISH

Made in United States
Troutdale, OR
08/28/2023